M000279363

"I learned how to better communicate with my diminishing, 86 year old mother who had advanced dementia. Their booklet helped my siblings and me to understand her language and her needs more empathetically and patiently. We became better caregivers for having read this memoir."

Laura J. Bernard
Dr. Gregory Keyes Medical Group

"My father was in declining health, exhibiting symptoms of dementia and potentially, Alzheimer's, and frankly I was uncomfortable with the whole experience. A friend gave me a copy of this book and then he gave me some really good advice, and suggested that I read it several times in advance of a visit with my father. The words of encouragement and advice have proved to be very helpful to my family and to me as we go through this experience."

Robert M. Ling, Jr.
President, Unified Grocers, Inc.

Remember, "I Can't Remember"

Shifting Your Paradigm
Reapproaching
Alzheimer's/Dementia

Eric Andersen
Heather Andersen

All rights reserved. No part of this book shall be reproduced or transmitted in any form or by any means, electronic, mechanical, magnetic, photographic including photocopying, recording or by any information storage and retrieval system, without prior written permission of the publisher. No patent liability is assumed with respect to the use of the information contained herein. Although every precaution has been taken in the preparation of this book, the publisher and author assume no responsibility for errors or omissions. Neither is any liability assumed for damages resulting from the use of the information contained herein.

Copyright © 2014 by Eric Andersen & Heather Andersen

ISBN 978-1-4958-0194-5 Softcover Black and White
ISBN 978-1-4958-0073-3 Softcover Color
ISBN 978-1-4958-0074-0 Hardcover Color
ISBN 978-1-4958-0075-7 eBook

Printed in the United States of America

Published July 2014

INFINITY PUBLISHING
1094 New DeHaven Street, Suite 100
West Conshohocken, PA 19428-2713
Toll-free (877) BUY BOOK
Local Phone (610) 941-9999
Fax (610) 941-9959
Info@buybooksontheweb.com
www.buybooksontheweb.com

In loving memory of

Helen Morris

January 28, 1912–January 28, 2007

"We cannot control the aging process of our loved ones...

What we can control
is
our response
to it."

Eric Andersen

Preface

We are thrilled to have this opportunity to present our book, but as I was thinking about what to say, I felt some trepidation that perhaps what we're saying is too simple and too insignificant. Then we decided that *that* is actually the book's strength. Our book is more of a booklet and is barely fifty pages. In terms of size, it's definitely insignificant, but anyone can read it because we are all capable of the insignificant. The best caregivers focus on achieving just that. They don't have to be doctors or pharmacists. They just have to religiously complete the most basic tasks, and that is where all their power lies. There is little glory in the tasks themselves, but honoring those simple things gives life. Become an expert on the insignificant.

There are many people to thank. I have to praise my in-laws, Gary and Lila Morris, for their willingness to move Grandma Helen from Colorado to their home. Also—and this underlines that *you cannot do this on your own*— many thanks to our dear friend and nurse practitioner, Becky Zambito, who was always a phone call away, giving us endless advice, love and encouragement. Thanks also to our family and friends, who supported us and saw

Grandma as a vital, participating part of our lives. Heartfelt thanks and gratitude to Casey Pratt for believing in this book and for taking it to the next level and to Susan Lenihan, our editor, for her encouragement and valuable insight.

We did not come quickly to this. When Gary and Lila first expressed their desire to care for Helen, we thought they were making a mistake. We thought it was better to leave her care to the experts because she wouldn't know where she was anyway. Also, we thought the return on the investment of their energy would be too little. There were endless phrases that seemed to make so much sense. This should be their time, etc. But they were undaunted, and they moved Grandma into their home.

It was a lot of work and required a great deal of energy, probably too much, so Heather, my "silent partner" and coauthor, started to go out to her parents' home one day a week to help with Grandma's needs until we moved her into our home. Heather took the lead in all that we have written here. She is a fantastic communicator and proved to be remarkably adept at working with Grandma. All the negatives that we have written were things I once spoke myself, and I was proven wrong on every one of them. So when I speak about caregiving, I am speaking about a transforming act. A caregiver should emerge changed.

The paradigm shift is that much of this is about you. The relationship between caregiver and loved one holds a great power. We generally think of caregiving as something that happens outside of ourselves. We are facilitating their journey and taking care of their needs, but the relationship is reciprocal and holds something for you as well. It is also *our* journey, and profound, deep changes and growth can take place within us.

During the caregiving process, we read Dr. Dean Ornish's wonderful book, *Love and Survival.* It made us realize the powerful impact the simplest acts of love can have on the human body. Our hope is that this book emphasizes the power of love and the value of maintaining the most human relationships all the way to the end. Phrases in our book are meant to be helpful to you immediately in a practical way and to turn your attention to the spiritual current that runs beneath all that we do. On the surface, simple, almost insignificant acts that carry deeply profound power make up life's final stage. We encourage you to not underestimate your significance.

By no means do I want to discount the pain, grief, and sadness that can accompany Alzheimer's/dementia. Your situation is unique, as are your characters and your setting. I am not an expert on your situation, but I became one on mine and I strongly encourage you to do the same.

My wife's grandmother, Helen, lived with us for two and a half years. She had dementia and required full-time care. All of her liquids had to be thickened, and she had to be spoon-fed. She became more work than we ever would have imagined, and she helped us grow in ways that we would never have predicted.

My wife and I developed Remember, I Can't Remember cards after a hospital/nursing home stay of Helen's. She had developed a blood clot in her lower leg. Our first thought was, "We get a little break. She will be in good hands at the hospital."

We filled out the form, indicating that she had full dementia, could not feed herself, and needed any liquids thickened. When we stopped by the next morning, her food tray had been removed because she had not touched it. Her water had not been thickened, and the breathing specialist was mentioning to her that her treatment would be the same as yesterday.

The next week at the nursing home, the aid was going to teach her how to get out of bed. In order to be taught, one needs to have memory. True, an elderly person with dementia becomes like a child, with one huge exception; we are always teaching and training children, but people with advanced dementia/Alzheimer's cannot be taught or trained. We created the card to remind the staff that she had no memory.

Doctors, nurses, and nursing aids were not grasping the significance of not remembering. Something else that seemed to be shocking to them was that she was thriving, quite happy, healthy, and clean. Generally, as the memory or mind changes, care diminishes. So much of our relationships are built on memory and name recognition that when those two things slide, highly attentive care often goes with them. Does the person even know? When a person loses their memory and their ability to perceive context, they have lost the ability to be their own advocate.

So this person, who no longer recognizes you as their child, does not know your name, and cannot remember that you visited yesterday, needs you now more than ever.

How do we relate to this new phase of growth? First, we do not consider it growth. To our eyes, the body and mind are deteriorating, so we see no growth. What about the parts we cannot see? The soul. I believe that there is a lot of activity and growth there.

We are so task-oriented, our value so tied to production, that it is very difficult to just be — to sit with someone and not get the recognition we are used to or to just sit and hold hands and visibly not accomplish anything. We can be so distracted that we rarely have time to recognize that our parent or loved one still has a voice and still has something to express. We have so many goals that get in the way of love.

We are so busy, and when someone like Helen no longer recognizes us or doesn't act the way that we are used to, it is an opportunity to decrease the energy and make our love a memory rather than a vital, life-changing force. We begin to decrease the power so that we won't be hurt, won't be caught off-guard, or waste our time. By loving what was, we become blind to what *is*. I truly believe that it takes an entire lifetime to live a life. Not one year short of, or six months less than. If we are still here, there must be something left for someone to do.

And what is this work to us? Another task, another obligation? Are we bystanders or unwilling participants who will do what is required? I believe that the process and our involvement in it is as much about us as it is about them. We can be moved by this and fundamentally altered. Aging and dying is transformation. It can be very messy and terribly inconvenient, but it is remarkably powerful, and, at times, beautiful.

We are working to conceive a play that illustrates the possible vision of a person with Alzheimer's/dementia. To the caretaker, she is an old woman sitting in a chair or lying on a bed. But through her eyes and those of the audience, she is a young woman with a husband and children. The children and husband are not cloudy vapors; they are solid and engaging. And they are not there to welcome her to the other side. They are just there, living with her. In the midst of this, we arrive with our schedule. We are going to get her to the bathroom. So the elderly woman feels a pull on her arm. Meanwhile, the young woman, in her mind, just sent her husband off to work and now has to get the kids to school. Suddenly she hears, "Come on, Mom. I have to get you to the bathroom."

She's thinking, "'Mom'?" This woman is older than I am. Why would she call me 'Mom'?"

And then with more urgency, we may say, "Mom, I don't have time for this today." The point of the play would be to show the growth of the characters, show the transforming power of aging, and most of all, reveal that their visions are not wispy vapors that respond to our schedules but are as concrete to them as our own lives are to us.

I am not pro-death or pro-dementia. I just argue for our involvement. I work to create a proactive response to aging. We cannot control the aging process of our loved ones. *What we can control is our response to it.* Caregiving is as much about the caregiver as it is about the patient. Caregiving is not about being a bystander but instead, being a proactive participant who may be altered or transformed.

My hope is that you will find this helpful, either as an aid for self-reflection or as the starting point for what can be very challenging conversations. You may not agree with everything written here, but if these points can generate dialogue, I will be satisfied.

Find a space to grieve.

This situation reveals the limits of our vocabulary. This is an ending. And because they are still with you, it may feel premature. The familiar roles are ending. Many aspects of your relationship that you took for granted are gone. This person looks like your loved one but is experiencing profound change. Recognize that there is sadness and anger. You will need help, and may return to this space often.

Then begin again.

With Alzheimer's/dementia, there are endless opportunities to begin again. I understand the pain and grief that accompanies this situation, but as we grieve for the person and the roles that were so familiar to us, we also have to open up to a new relationship with new roles and new opportunities. I believe our presence and commitment in these times speaks volumes on a soul level. You are still a son or daughter, but it is possible that what is needed of you transcends those labels.

Do not remind them that they can't remember.

Reminding them they can't remember will only cause them anxiety and will be a waste of your energy. Their inability to remember will, at times, make you angry and cause great frustration, but understand that it is beyond their control. They cannot try harder and they cannot prioritize. When we forget a name or lose our keys, we can go into a mind space and usually find what we are looking for. They have lost that ability and generally cannot remember what they forgot. Directing your frustration toward them is, at the very least, counter-productive.

Constantly remind yourself that they can't remember.

The seemingly simple task of remembering they can't remember will cause a paradigm shift. Do not read anything into it. They really just can't remember. Take the time to consider what that means. It means they cannot follow your lengthy explanation of what short-term memory loss is. It means they have lost their ability to manipulate you. They cannot be trained or taught to take their medicine or drink their water. They cannot remember what you just said no matter how loudly or slowly you said it. Their forgetting does not diminish the previous value of any person, relationship, experience, or thing. We do not want to believe that we are so easily forgotten. We may get resentful and angry. We have an intense need to be acknowledged and remembered. Usually we view it as their anger lashing out with a combative spirit, when, at least in part, it may be ours. They simply can't remember. How much of the Alzheimer's/dementia struggle is about us? How much of their struggle comes from our anxiety? We need to be willing to move toward the unknown.

Accepting this is accepting their loss and our loss. It represents a shift in the relationship that we may not be ready for. That acceptance may be heartbreaking, but it is the starting point for care.

Let go of your name and expand your identity.

We are afraid to leave our name. We fear leaving the old dynamic of our relationship. Our clinging solely to the roles of the past inhibits the growth or evolution of our relationship. We have to trust enough to meet them where they are. Our relationship may shift from one grounded in current events and past experiences to a relationship of souls. That is a great leap.

Work to understand their anger.

We hear a lot about combative and angry Alzheimer's/dementia experiences. We consider that anger to be a symptom of Alzheimer's/dementia. But how angry can *we* get when we can't find our keys or when we forget to make a deposit, pay a bill, or keep an appointment? Imagine the frustration when you can't find your life, or when an older woman approaches you and claims to be the daughter that you just saw run out the door in a little dress and pigtails. You might be enjoying a game of cards when a man, roughly the age of your husband, whom you have not been able to locate, grips your arm and says, "Mom, it's time to go to the bathroom."

Work to understand your anger.

This is the beginning of the last stage of life. The two of you may have unresolved issues. You may feel cheated that you did not have your time to say your piece. Caregiving is not the appropriate forum to bring up past slights and reignite past anger.

Contemplate forgiveness.

This final stage may last several months. It may last many years. There may be things you can do to make their final transition easier. You can view this time as pointless, cruel, or unfair. All of those options have very valid arguments, but you can also see it as another stage of life that may hold some value. This work is very difficult if you do it from a place of anger or resentment. There may be past hurts or serious falling-outs; work to let go of the anger and blame that may be left. Work to forgive.

Meet them where they are.

Enter into their reality. Remember, it is as real to them as ours is to us. I believe we are mistaken when we think that our arrival, or our voice, has the immediate power to pull them from a world of ghost-like vapors back to our concrete world. We have to value the unseen and at least accept the powerful effect it has on them. Our flippant disregard for what they experience unfortunately does not make it go away. Their visions are very real to them and create feelings of real joy or real sadness. Listen to them and comfort them. Respect where they are.

Seek help. Provide help. Be united.

This can be exhausting work. You are going to need help. Hopefully, there are other family members willing to contribute time or resources. Not everyone has the same skill set, and many are not comfortable with the intimacy that this work entails. Give the gift of working a little beyond your comfort level. If you absolutely cannot contribute in physical ways, be creative and search for other ways to lessen the burden.

Make this an all-inclusive experience.

Include your children. Try to look at this as a part of life, not something that takes one away from life. If the grandchildren are young, they can learn a great deal from your modeling. They can gain insight into the ways we define life and its value. The joy of children is a great gift to the elderly. If they are adults, they may be able to shoulder much of the caregiving without the same friction that often exists between child and parent.

There may be no I in we, but in caregiving, there is usually a we in I.

Throughout this book we have used I instead of we, because it reads better and is less confusing, but there was never a moment of I alone. Caring for Helen took Heather's and my full commitment. Understand that there is no doing this alone. Even if you are shouldering all the work, those around you will affected, and for you to be successful they will have to pitch in to cover your previous responsibilities or will be asked to forgive your ability to do so. Caregiving is a noble undertaking, but it requires sacrifices by you and those around you.

You do not need the last word.

Something that Alzheimer's/dementia renders completely irrelevant is the last word. Do not argue. As a caregiver, you have goals and priorities, but you may need to change your style of communicating to achieve those goals. There is no room for your ego. The analogy of the iron fist wrapped in an extremely soft glove might apply here. Your goal may be getting their pills down or getting them to drink their water. These seemingly simple tasks may require all of your powers of persuasion, endless re-approaching and some manipulation, but there is no room for anger, and direct conflict becomes silly.

Let go of current events.

Focus on other topics of discussion. This is where your knowledge of your loved one's past is so important. Linear time has no hold on the Alzheimer's/dementia experiencer. Physicists have said for years that linear time is a construct of our minds to organize our world. Your loved one's world may seem to be happening all at once, with childhood memories mingling with adult and both bleeding into present day. Observe. Let yourself be curious. Loosen your grip and let them go. I know that seems counterintuitive, but it works. It is very hard to let someone go and still take care of his or her every need.

Let go of your name. You are so much more.

Dealing with memory loss forces us to consider the essence of who we are. We often find that so much of our value is tied to the past that we are unable to travel into the future without it. When a loved one begins to forget the names of family and friends, it is a point of crisis. I have heard so many times, "When my mother/father/grandmother/ friend forgot my name, she died to me. She was no longer that person to me." Is our being really that tied to our name? We should consider how much value we place on it. I think we would argue that our self is more than our name, but when a loved one forgets it, our self is threatened, and their self is gone.

Contemplate unconditional love.

Be Mindful of the energy you bring.

Nothing contributes more to their calmness than your calmness. The same is true of anxiety or resentment.

You do not need to win.

There will be endless opportunities for arguing. Let go of your need to win.

Touch them.

In an Alzheimer's/dementia caregiving situation, touch can say so much more than words. Just sitting and holding their hand or rubbing lotion on their skin can often be more powerful and healing than any conversation. Our lives are so geared toward accomplishment and action that being calm and still can be challenging, if not impossible, for many. They have lost memory, but they can still sense energy and respond strongly to the energy you bring.

Forgive.

There is no good time for the onset of Alzheimer's/ dementia. There are often unresolved issues that need to be released. That is the work, the releasing and the forgiving. Work on it.

This is about you.

The paradigm shift is the realization that much of this is about you. As a caregiver, you cannot control the way your loved one acts. What you can control is how you respond to them. **Remember, they can't remember**. This is not as simple as it sounds.

The only consistency is inconsistency.

Really. This is why Alzheimer's/dementia experiencers often suffer in facilities. They are constantly changing their sleep habits, eating habits, and bathroom times. The caregiver has to be flexible. If your loved one is in an elder care facility, you may have to pitch in to cover the gaps created by their changing habits. There may be times when they sleep until two o'clock in the afternoon; as challenging as it is, their meal times and medicine schedule has to change with them.

Schedules do not work. It is not personal.

Our lives run clockwise. We are always mindful of the time. Theirs run counterclockwise. Time is completely irrelevant. It took us a long time to accept that we had to have a very loose schedule. If we planned a night out or day away, invariably Grandma would be on a different schedule. This is why extra help is so necessary. Every caregiver needs someone who can step in and complete the tasks (feeding, walking, changing, bathing) so they can still occasionally adhere to some sort of schedule. If you are approaching caregiving with a strong schedule in mind, be prepared for a rude awakening.

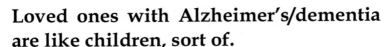

Loved ones with Alzheimer's/dementia are like children, sort of.

They can be like children or infants in their total dependence on you or their approach to the world and by their ability to cause you great frustration without intending to. They differ greatly from children in that they are not learning or absorbing and moving toward independence. They are forgetting and becoming less mobile and more dependent. They cannot be taught. Accept that.

Be grateful for the opportunity to start again and again and again.

They may ask you about their breakfast before and after each bite. They may ask you when you are coming back or where you have been. Remember, they can't remember. You can accept that and answer patiently, or you can fight it each time. It is your energy. Be mindful that the energy you send to them will quickly return to you. Take responsibility and consider why you are so frustrated. The phrase, "as you give, so will you receive" is very true in this relationship.

Home is not an actual address.

Imagine being in a room that may seem a bit familiar to you, but you don't actually recognize anything in it. Now imagine that you have people walking in and out of your space. If there is no acknowledgment, you begin to feel that you don't belong and that you are in the way. All they can think of is going home. Where is home? They have no idea, but what they do know is the feeling of belonging, and I believe that is what home represents to them. They are searching for a feeling more than a place.

Do not ask pointed questions that require lengthy explanations.

Allow them the opportunity to cover up or disguise their forgetfulness. They realize that something is amiss; do not pressure them for specifics.

Do not confuse them with choices.

Know their likes and dislikes. It is a balancing act, allowing for their autonomy, but also taking the initiative and freeing them from what can be an anxiety-causing process.

It may be helpful to think of dementia as "dimensia," meaning a problem with dimensions.

At times we may appear to be in contrary dimensions, both having an equal hold. The challenge is to gracefully, or at least effectively, bridge that gap.

Do not hesitate to lie.

In this situation, lying makes your life and theirs so much easier. If you are struggling with a moral position, you are going to have to let it go. They are only spending a part of their time in our reality; telling them our truths may actually be cruel and may show an inability on your part to let go. They may not remember the truths you just told them, but the anxiety those truths cause will stick with them.

Present things as their idea.

"You mentioned to me that you wanted to get an early start today." "You were saying that you might like some help with your hair." As a caregiver, you have to be very creative.

Deflect. Next to patience, the ability to deflect criticism or divert attention is your greatest tool.

They will have many moments of high anxiety, and they will be set on things that are no longer possible for them. Realize that they are losing the ability to fixate, focus, or argue. They are changing rapidly. The solution to many issues is to divert their attention and wait them out. Try to avoid direct arguments. Remember that you have the upper hand and be resourceful.

Do not try to explain too much. Remember, they can't remember.

Any lengthy explanation will lead to them forgetting the original subject. Conserve your energy and spare them the confusion. Volume and enunciation do not help.

Short-term memory loss means short-term memory loss.

Deal with the now. The responsibility to remember is yours.

Do not try to train or teach. It will not work.

No matter how much you want it to, they really just do not have the capacity to retain the information. Their learning would simplify your life but so would accepting that they can't be taught.

Spoil them.

Basic nutrition is, of course, important, but there will be times when it will be very difficult to get them to eat anything. Assuming they are not diabetic, let them eat what they will. There may be days when they eat lots of pudding. The days of having to eat their vegetables should be over. At this stage, it really doesn't matter so much what they eat as long as they do eat and drink.

Experiment with the power of love.

There really is no greater medicine for either one of you. It is a great gift to be able to love without limits.

Do not expect gratitude for specific actions.

It is not that they don't appreciate what you do for them. They just can't remember you did it or what was done. It is very challenging when your many contributions go unnoticed. In life, we are so conscious of reward and gratitude. It doesn't mean we are selfish or shallow. It is just how most of life works. It is so natural to say, "She won't know anyway." With the Alzheimer's/dementia experiencer, the majority of what you do will never be recognized, but I believe that energy is not wasted. The act of doing is transforming.

Focus on what they are, not what they are not.

It is easy to see what they are no longer. Give them the gift of recognizing what they are right now. This is the last stage of a long life. Contrary to appearances, I believe there is a lot going on. (Receiving care, understanding vulnerability, teaching you, and releasing control)

Listen. They may have something to teach you.

Do not discount everything they say. They may shock you with insights and an awareness that you would not expect.

Be conscious of their physical complaints.

There will be times when you do not want to hear it, but do not discount their physical complaints. Bladder infections and dehydration are very common and can show up as lack of appetite, constipation, achy pains, or nausea.

You will feel sorry for yourself.

Why me? may come up more than you would like to admit.

Know yourself. You may not be able to do this. Accept that and quickly find somebody who can.

Every relationship is unique. Some move into the caregiver mode more naturally than others do. Work on opening up to different care scenarios. It does not have to be all or nothing. No matter where your loved one is, you can still contribute. In addition to relationship challenges, there may also be physical limitations. Helen weighed eighty-six pounds; her small stature made in-home caregiving possible. In many situations, this is not the case.

It is very challenging to be a caregiver, but for many, it is equally challenging to be cared for.

Being fully dependent is many people's worst fear. We tend to think that the one receiving the care is on the easy end, but receiving care can be very challenging. Most of us have lived our lives with a strong desire for independence and a fear of ever being a "burden" for our children.

What can I do when they ask the same question again and again?

Not much. Go outside and take some deep breaths. Recognize how short their retention span is. Asking the same question is a symptom of short-term memory loss. Answering them sternly or harshly does not help. You cannot make them remember. The onus of memory is on us. Work on accepting that. Notes may help early on, but as Alzheimer's/dementia progresses, the notes are seen out of context. How can I get her to remember to take her pills? You can't. At a certain point, that is no longer their responsibility, and the question becomes, "How am I going to give her her pills? How am I going to remember to get her water?"

In spite of, and because of, all they are going through, they may actually be happy. Try not to hold that against them.

You may resent them for not fighting. It is devastating to feel your loved one slipping away without a fight. In their position, fighting may not be possible. They cannot try harder to remember. They cannot work at being better. They are not capable of holding that concept in their head long enough to achieve it. You may begrudge them their happiness when they are also unaware of your struggles. Be grateful for their contentment. Our lives have too little of that.

Laugh!

Much of this is actually quite funny. You have to maintain your sense of humor. Don't be afraid to laugh. Laughter is contagious and so is tension. Err on the side of laughter.

Be accommodating.

At the advanced stage, the Alzheimer's/dementia experiencers needs are many, but their wants are few. Helen got tremendous joy from the simplest of things; the sun on her face, the wind in her hair on a Sunday drive. Providing life's simple pleasures can be so easy for us and so impactful to them. Throughout our lives we often feel ineffective; putting out great effort and affecting little change. Within your relationship with the

Alzheimer's/dementia experiencer there will be moments where you can affect great change with the slightest of efforts. Often while feeding Helen her dinner, she would stop between bites, sweep her arm across the table and say, What about all of these people? Who will feed them?" And then go further, with growing concern saying, "Is there enough for everyone?" I would say, "Oh Grandma, there is plenty for everyone. Heather is in the kitchen preparing theirs. We did not expect them, but we have plenty." In that beautiful little exchange, her concerns vanished and I actually felt like I accomplished something.

You have great power.

Do not underestimate it. Utilize it and contemplate ways of realizing it.

You already possess most of what they need.

In addition to love, the core of this experience is accessing or discovering those traits or attributes that you already possess.

Do not ever assume that you know when it is their time to go.

Regardless of medical advances and spiritual development, death is still a great mystery and we are blind to many of its elements. Be respectful of its mystery.

For bathing, use the guidelines of do unto others.

Hydrate them, always.

It is difficult, but not half as difficult as it is if you don't. Know the warning signs for dehydration. Be aware of their medications. Many prescribed drugs act as diuretics.

Do not hesitate to call a doctor.

Be conscious of a rapid decline in physical abilities and mental clarity. For the most part, Alzheimer's/dementia is a relatively slow disease. If you are noticing rapid changes, there may be a problem with their medication mix, oxygen levels or dehydration and/or bladder infection.

They have great value.

However, it may not be obvious to everyone. It is unfortunate, or just reality, but you establish the value of your loved one. You are the model. If you are attentive, compassionate and engaged in their well-being, it is much more likely that the doctors, nurses and other family members will be also.

Do not patronize.

Be conscious of eye rolling and talking down to, as a caregiver. Approach your care receiver with respect and curiosity. No matter how cute, sweet and grandma-like someone may appear, they should never be patronized.

Fight for their health.

Do not let go until they do.

Take responsibility.

Because no one else will. No one else has the full-picture; caregiver, family, doctor, housing, diet, medical history, idiosyncrasies. See yourself as the project manager overseeing many sub-contractors, just as electricians may not know what the plumbers are doing, or vice-versa, nor will they care. There will be occasions when you will be disappointed that a doctor, or sibling or specialist missed something – it's going to happen. Despite much effort, it is not a perfect system.

Be an advocate. They need you or someone very much like you.

They can no longer take care of themselves. They don't know what is best for them. It is hard to find other people who care enough to always do what is right.

The hospital is not an inherently safe place.

If your loved one has a stay in the hospital, do not see it as a break from your responsibility. You should know your loved one better than the doctor and the nurses do. You know their idiosyncrasies and their specific needs. Often, the nurses are exhausted, and the doctors are too busy. There are constant shift changes. Things are missed, and information is not passed on. You have to demand good care and be willing to pick up the slack. Take responsibility for their medicine and their liquids. Helen had a doctor who was a dementia expert. The only problem was that he had no actual interest in seeing her. Fortunately, in time, we found a highly attentive doctor who combined expertise with a great bedside manner.

Knowing how much medication (i.e., sedatives) to give is difficult and very personal. Don't immediately accept every evaluation.

When we receive a prescription for ourselves, the pharmacist will review the side effects and dosage requirements and we partially listen, thinking, "Yeah, yeah, I get it. Take with water." With the Alzheimer's/dementia experiencer we do not have the luxury of half-listening. Their body may be frail, their health compromised and they do not have the ability to clearly verbalize what might be wrong. In this condition, side effects may have a huge impact on their overall health and well-being.

Cry when they are gone. Be engaged enough in the experience that you are not just putting in the time.

Don't keep them at arm's length. Literally, roll up your sleeves and get involved. You will hear that it's for the best, etc., and it may be, but be involved enough to really feel the experience.

Do not believe statistics or timetables.

Every situation is unique and personal. Good, attentive care renders many statistics irrelevant.

Express sincere gratitude.

Express sincere love.

Try to know them.

This is an opportunity to know your loved one without the same structure of your previous roles. You may gain glimpses of their childhood, and you might discover a vulnerability that was never exposed to you. Although everything you know is rapidly changing, this may be an opportunity to actually know your parent.

Value this time. There is something here for you.

Give them the acceptance you hope for.

Let go of baggage.

Do not be afraid.

When this work is over, know there will be a peculiar void.

Value the unseen.

Silence is okay.

Support their dignity. It does matter how they look.

We cannot emphasize enough the power you have as a caregiver. By just obsessively doing the simplest tasks of feeding, hydrating, bathing and knowing them and their routines, you contribute more to their health than any "expert" can. You must be the advocate. Only you will know what is normal. Commit to those tasks, and you are giving the greatest gift you may ever give. Be conscious, and you will receive in equal measure.

Call on the grandchildren and everyone else.

Of all family members, the grandchildren may have the easiest time with the changes that accompany dementia. Adult grandchildren may also be the most capable caregivers. They have the most energy and the least baggage. Consider that option.

Bathe them often.

They will be so much more approachable.

They need water—lots of it.

It is very important to know that if your loved one becomes dehydrated, you cannot rehydrate them. They must go to the hospital. With any elderly person, it is very important to monitor their liquid intake.

They need love—lots of it.

Protect them.

Know them.

Trust yourself.

You know your loved one better than anyone else—including the doctors.

In the center of obligation, search for joy and choice and try to work from there.

Do not do this on your own.

Share the burden and the gift.

Epilogue to a Very Satisfying Life.

She could have died two years ago at the end of a very satisfying life, but instead, she hung around at heaven's doorway and gave us the most beautiful gift we could ever receive. She gave us the gift of unconditional love and she gave us a chance to love without restraint.

We will miss all the activity around her. She was always entertaining, directing, sharing and often commented on the beautiful, bright light in the room. She loved to look at it, marvel at its beauty, but until her ninety-fifth birthday, was never inclined to follow it.

She lived a beautiful love story. Her husband was always with her. She was often talking about her children. What are they doing? Were they alright? At times, she was an old woman; and the next minute, she was a young woman with children, or a child herself, asking for her dad.

A woman considered to no longer be in her right mind that never forgot to be kind, polite, gracious, and thankful. We are struck dumb.

We are always seeking in art, architecture, and nature that quality without a name that strikes you at the soul and moves your heart. You can't describe it, but you know exactly what it feels like. We were lucky enough to live with Grandma, a woman who fully embodied that quality. What we will miss the most is that quality that can't be named. She filled our lives with it. Looking at her face was like seeing God so thinly veiled, and we could not turn our eyes away. We had to smell her hair and kiss her face. We were transfixed and endlessly fascinated. A misperception is that when you care for someone so intimately, your world becomes so small, but when we would grasp her hand, our world expanded to the infinite. We will miss that.

After ninety-two years, you generally stop impressing people, and you don't gather a lot of new friends. Add full dementia to that equation and your life can seem pretty insignificant, but she kept on gathering. She may not have realized it consciously, but she sensed it and knew that she was loved by many. She continued to radiate love to all who met her and gained friends and inspired people until the very end.

We just came across a scribbled note of one of our conversations with Grandma. It began with me asking her if she knew she was a blessing every day.

She replied with this: "That is because you see the parts of me that I can't see." She went on to say, "We go through our lives and learn so little of what we are supposed to learn. From the time that we are infants on up, we learn and are taught the wrong things. We need some of it, but it is not what is really important. I am really trying to learn that now. We only see such a small part of who we really are." I wonder, can someone be ninety-five years old and still be wise beyond their years?

To quote a favorite song lyric, "The greatest thing you'll ever learn is just to love and be loved in return." ("Nature Boy," written by Eden Ahbez) And that was our life with Grandma Helen. Every morning, she was a bright light of pure joy. "Aren't we lucky? We are so blessed. Isn't it beautiful?" She must have said those things a dozen times each day. Caregiving at times was very taxing, and often we just felt incredibly exhausted, but then we'd go up to her and say, "Hello, beautiful." Her face would light up with a beaming smile. She'd squeeze our hands, our hearts would rise and for that moment our fatigue would disappear. She was like magic. How could we be so lucky? She was truly our blessing. God sent us our own angel, a tiny little eighty-six-pound lady with dementia. How amazing is that?

Write your own story. . . . .

Care Planning Guide

I like that ending – write your own story. Take what you can from ours, but write your own. But where to begin? Most of these stories begin accidentally and without warning, or maybe with a little warning that can easily be overlooked until it is too late and suddenly we are frantic.

As I think of ways to start a story, two distinctly different approaches come to mind. One is the classic opening line of myths, fables and folklore, "Once upon a time..." and the other is, the famous first sentence, "It was a dark and stormy night..." from English novelist Edward Bullwer-Lytton's novel, *Paul Clifford*. In our pre-crisis minds, the once upon a time seems perfectly plausible. There is a predictable reading, there is resolution and all the characters play their expected roles. The ending is foretold and usually involves "and they all lived happily ever after." Or, as written in the original version, they all lived happily until their deaths.

With, *it was a dark and stormy night*, we know we will be in for a heck of a ride that will challenge us in unpredictable ways and there is no guaranteed outcome. Given the choice we would opt out of this scenario, which is why this particular storyline always catches us unawares.

That famous opening line goes further, "The rain fell in torrents-except at occasional intervals, when it was checked by a violent gust of wind which swept up the streets, rattling along the housetops, and fiercely agitating the scanty flame of the lamps that struggled against the darkness." That line is pretty accurate in it's description of the feelings of many in the midst of an Alzheimer's/dementia crisis and yes, I still say enter into this – there is something here for you, but bring a suitcase, and maybe a little preparation, and planning would prove helpful. Perhaps, by approaching your story more like a novel, a fairytale ending will be more likely.

We love to watch movies about this life stuff, but it is very difficult to live it. Caregiving for an Alzheimer's/dementia experiencer is not a sprint, it is more like a marathon, broken into unexpected periods of sprinting, undertaken by a non-runner, unsure whether he is running to or from.

I had a business idea. Actually, I have had many, but I knew people would flock to this one. I would act as a facilitator and discuss the issues of aging before they needed to be discussed and develop family care plans before they needed to be activated. Being an outside voice I thought I could bring up those topics that are so hard to voice within families. Well, there was no flocking to, or door pounding, because with an outsider or just among family, we do not want to discuss these things. Some of it may be superstition; things are going so well, let's not jinx it. Or, it seems like we just emerged from the struggles of growing up, now this?!

Some of you may have spent the last twenty or thirty years working to keep your family out of your business and yourself out of theirs. If that is the case this will be challenging.

Tolstoy said, "All happy families resemble one another and each unhappy family is unhappy in its own way." I will borrow that phrase and reiterate that your story will be unique. Of all the families I have come across that are facing the issues of Alzheimer's/dementia they are all dealing with their own set of unique problems and hopefully, in time, arriving at their own set of unique solutions.

A little conversation can take you a long way; a lot of conversation can take you much further. There is much to be discussed between siblings and between siblings and parents.

Know that this experience may not go as originally planned, you may need Plan B before you even begin Plan A, but do not get discouraged; be open to the process, control the things you can and keep a very watchful eye on the things you can't.

Discuss different care scenarios-
What is adequate care?
    A. Your parent's vision
    B. Your vision
    C. Siblings vision

How does your parent envision his/her future?
How do you see it?
What is your role in it?

Are there care options?
    A. Long-term care insurance
    B. Local care facilities
    C. One or more siblings he/she could live with
    D. Living at home with in-home care
    E. Group home
    F. Pros and cons of each.

When looking at different care option prices, closely examine what is included in the monthly price and what is considered an extra. **Do not assume anything.**

If he/she has an accident or an injury, what are the rehab/convalescent options?

In the case of an emergency, who will take the lead in communicating with doctors, rehab/convalescent centers and caregivers?

Does everyone have knowledge of prescriptions/allergies, medical history?

What is DNR?

Do they have a living will?

Establish a monthly communication schedule to assess changes. A family member that lives away may think that is excessive, a family member in the midst of caring may want weekly communication or vice versa.

Siblings may be scattered all across the globe, and if that is the case, you need to find a local contact that can keep you informed of changes.

If your loved one is in a care facility, VISIT, more than you think you need to. Their care will be better, because of it.

Develop an emergency plan. If an accident occurs and your loved one goes to the hospital, they will generally need a place (care facility, rehab, family home) to go within three to four days.

Is Medicaid an option?

If in-home living is an option, what needs to be done to the home?

When hiring a caregiver, who will take the lead in the interviewing and hiring? Once hired there should be a designated individual responsible for caregiver salary and addressing any concerns that will arise.

Be conscious of changes in your loved one; do not discount what they say, but do not take it all as gospel either. There may be accusations that arise out of a need to make sense of a situation that they cannot understand. Family members or caregivers may be accused of stealing or other transgressions.

These accusations are always worthy of investigation, but keep an open mind. If handled hastily, these situations can cause irreparable fallout.

The group Aging with Dignity (agingwith dignity.org) created what has been called "the living will with a heart and soul." It contains the following five wishes.

Wish 1: The person I want to make decisions for me when I can't.

This section is an assignment of a health care agent. This person makes medical decisions on your behalf if you are unable to speak for yourself.

Wish 2: The kind of medical treatment I want or don't want.

This section is a living will—a definition of what life support means to you, and when you would and would not want it.

Wish 3: How comfortable I want to be.

This section addresses matters of comfort and care—what type of pain management you would like.

Wish 4: How I want people to treat me.

This section speaks to personal matters, such as whether you would like to be at home, desire bedside prayer and other matters of spirituality.

Wish 5: What I want my loved ones to know.

This section is very personal, dealing with matters of forgiveness and final wishes regarding funeral or memorial plans.

Keep putting yourself in their shoes. They are going through many struggles that we gloss over with, "Well, that is aging. That is what getting old is all about." That is true, but in our minds we are usually so much younger than we really are. Getting old can be a shock to everyone involved.

Failure to thrive is not uncommon.

At any other age, the problems of the aged would be viewed as catastrophic. They may have just lost their spouse, they have recently lost many lifelong friends, they can no longer drive and even walking takes great effort. Their list of ailments is lengthy. They have lived their lives full of expectation and eyes to the future, and then at some point their birthday's significance represents a subtraction from years left rather than an addition of things gained. That reads so heavy, but aging is not without casualties. They deserve our compassion, even if it is without our understanding.

Beware there may be money! Or there was money.

Nothing disrupts a good fairytale faster than the appearance or disappearance of money. Aging is expensive. Good care and poor care are expensive. Do your homework; abysmal care may cost more than excellent care. It is rarely cheaper.

A good rule of thumb....

The money, if there is any, is theirs until they are no longer.

Do the math

If a family member is being compensated for caregiving, do the math. Break the total down to an hourly rate. It is usually not as much as you think. Depending on the individual being cared for, caregiving may be a twenty-four hour a day undertaking. Going further, understand that if the family caregiver is hiring a capable substitute, the substitute will most likely charge a much higher hourly rate than the family member receives.

Who manages the resources?

When undertaking a family caregiving situation it is common to have one child as caregiver and one as money manager. That method is not wrong, but it does require a very conscious effort by both individuals to understand the role of the other. Where one may be envious of an opportunity to "stay home" the other may be envious of the ability to ever leave.

Master a skill…

…even if it is just taking your parent or grandparent to the bathroom.
In that way you are not unique, this makes everyone uncomfortable.

In caregiving all siblings are created equal.

Historically, caregiving duties have fallen quickly to the daughters, but that should no longer be the case. Try to see past traditional gender roles when dividing up the responsibilities and view each other as equal participants rather than sons and daughters.

Notes

Notes

Notes

Notes

CPSIA information can be obtained at www.ICGtesting.com
Printed in the USA
LVOW06s1340010914

401834LV00002BA/2/P